THE TELEMARK
SKI BOOK

THE TELEMARK SKI BOOK

An Introduction to Cross Country Downhill

BY JAY CARROLL AND GORDON HARDY

A Campbell-Merritt/Stephen Greene Press Book
Lexington, Massachusetts

Acknowledgments: Cover photograph of Kirstin Siebert by Hanson Carroll. All inside black-and-white photographs also by Hanson Carroll, except the photographs appearing in Chapter 4, which are by Steven Mooney. Thanks to James Rouse for consulting on material presented in Chapter 4. Thanks also to *Cross Country Skier* magazine and to Kate Hanson for helping produce this book. Karhu-Titan USA and the Merrell Boot Company provided equipment used in the photographs in Chapter 3.

First published in 1984

10 9 8 7 6 5 4 3

This book is manufactured in the United States of America. It is designed by Craig Woods and Mallory Phelps and published by The Stephen Greene Press, Lexington, Massachusetts.

Distributed by Viking Penguin Inc.

THE TELEMARK SKI BOOK

To all who love to ski

FOREWORD

It was one of those days: A bright February sun shone in an indigo sky and a fresh layer of dry, cold powder graced the Vermont ridges. We toured into the backcountry, savoring the afternoon like a connoisseur savors a rare wine. We convened finally at the top of a snowy slope. Jay Carroll was giving telemark lessons.

There were six of us in all, ages 25 to 55, on nordic ski gear that ranged from low- to mid-cut boots and from wood to metal-edge fiberglass skis. Most of us had alpine downhill skiing experience as well as cross country touring skills, and each wanted to experience the fluid grace of linking telemark turns down the slope. Jay is a natural athlete and a natural teacher, so we were in good hands. Gordon Hardy, who was turned on to telemarking in California's Sierra, was there to help, too.

When we finished with our hillside, its powder snow told a story of a lot of downhill—and uphill—runs. Before the afternoon gathered itself into dusk, however, Jay and Gordon had managed to get each of us to make at least one or two *bona fide* telemarks, to feel the grace with which ski edges, snow, and gravity can work together.

Telemark skiing is a way of going downhill on traditional nordic, free-heel gear. It is predicated on the graceful telemark turn, the execution of which is a broad challenge to both the cross country skier and the skilled alpine skier accustomed to lift-served slopes. What is happening in some sectors of the American skiing scene is that getting from the top of a hill to the bottom has become less important than the way in which you do it. Many skiers have recognized that to do it with the sweeping arcs of telemark turns is not only challenging and fun but, well, awfully damn classy, too.

This book is for the skier who wants to learn how to telemark ski. It is especially aimed at the skier who is planning to ski lift-served slopes, whether he be from a nordic or alpine skiing background. There are no chapters on winter camping or backcountry survival techniques in this book; those topics are covered admirably by other authors. What you'll find on the following pages is straightforward instruction on learning the telemark turn.

Had I a book such as this to read before my introduction to telemarking that February afternoon in Vermont, I know there would have been fewer personal imprints on that slope and more complete telemarks before the afternoon ended. But finally this book *has* come along, incorporating Jay's and Gordon's technical expertise and substantial writing and editing skills.

Which is good news for those of us skiers who welcome challenge, seek fun, and would get from the top of a hill to the bottom with a touch of class.

CRAIG WOODS
Putney, Vermont

THE TELEMARK
SKI BOOK

CHAPTER 1

INTRODUCTION TO
TELEMARKING

Telemark, Norway, is a region in the southern part of the Scandi- navian peninsula between Oslo and the Atlantic coast. Between its long rivers and deep lakes—the Tinnsjo, Nisser, and Norsja— nestle the rounded mountains and rolling hills characteristic of Eu- rope's northland. Winter comes early to these hills and lingers through the lengthening nights until well into the warming light of springtime.

Like all Norwegians, the people of Telemark are avid cross country skiers. First as a means of transport and later as a winter recreation, skiing has been a way of life to these people. Their skiing history stretch- es into the dimmest reaches of time and remains a tradition of pride and skill. Here, scratched in prehistoric petroglyphs, are figures of hunt- ers with long, curved skis on their feet. Here, too, tomorrow's champion skiers are born and nurtured in the traditions of a skiing people.

Being an out-of-the-way sort of place, Telemark might have remained obscure to the rest of the world had it not been for a style of ski turn invented here. But like the stem christy (named for the city of Chris- tiania, now Oslo), its name has been spread through the world by a home-grown invention—the telemark turn.

Webster's dictionary defines the telemark as "a turn in which the ski that is to be on the outside of the turn is advanced considerably ahead of the other ski and then turned inward at a steadily widening angle until the actual turn." That's a good description—for a dictionary—but any- one who has advanced a ski "considerably ahead of the other ski" can tell you that the telemark turn is more than just that. There is a special feel to telemark skiing, an elegant sense of control and coordination that's like no other form of skiing. It combines techniques and equip- ment of both cross country (or nordic) and downhill (or alpine) skiing, adding to those a few special elements all its own.

From downhill, telemark skiing adopts two things: the metal-edged ski and the force of gravity. Though not essential to telemark skiing, the metal edges of a telemark ski allow you to carve turns in the snow with

3

more ease and greater control than with an edgeless ski. The force of gravity, simply, is what pulls you down the hill, creating speed and acceleration. Telemarking takes a bit more from downhill skiing, of course, and if you're already a downhiller, you'll recognize some techniques of your sport in the telemark turn. Still, it's important not to think of telemarking as just "downhill skiing." It has its own technique, and the downhiller who tries to make the turn an imitation of alpine skiing may find it difficult to learn properly.

From cross country skiing, telemarking embraces the free-heel, toe-clip boot-and-binding system. This means lighter, more flexible equipment and greater freedom of movement when skiing. As with cross country track skiing, the free heel is the *sine qua non* of telemarking, allowing you to assume the proper stance for a controlled, graceful curve down the hill.

At its heart, telemark skiing converts two skis into one. That is, when you assume the basic telemark stance—one ski forward of the other, knees bent, with the tip of the back ski nestled close to the binding of the forward ski—you are in effect creating a single, arc-shaped ski. With this ski, you glide across and down the face of a hill, controlling your movement by altering the position of the arc relative to the slope of the hill. It's quite a balancing act at first—new telemarkers sometimes create more sitzmarks than turns on their first day. Once you get the hang of it, though, the turn is nothing short of exhilarating.

Norwegian immigrants probably brought the telemark turn with them when they settled the snowy regions of the United States. The turn's first public recognition came when skiers noticed Scandinavian ski jumpers using the turn for their landings. The telemark is highly suited to the needs of ski jumpers: It gives excellent stability upon landing because of its solid footing and resistance to forward pitch. Also, the turn creates good shock absorption, from the bent knees and ankles of the basic stance.

Much of the current interest in telemarking, though, originated not with ski jumpers, but with downhill skiers. In the mid-1970s, many alpine skiers were dissatisfied with their sport. The rise of alpine in the 1950s and 1960s had led to all sorts of advanced techniques and specialized equipment, making the sport ultrasophisticated and, incidentally, very expensive. Some skiers were becoming a trifle bored with the endless hairsplitting refinements of high-tech downhill. They were looking for a new thrill, and what they discovered was telemarking. Suddenly, these skiers had a new challenge.

Telemark skiing required a new look at their downhill technique. Moreover, it required new equipment—gear that was lighter, freer than the heavy metal they were used to bombing down the slopes on. The feeling of skiing was still there, but now these downhillers found something that gave them new challenge, new excitement, and new reward for their practice—a way to discover skiing all over again.

Cross country skiers, too, gravitated toward the "new" discipline of telemark skiing. Sometimes disdainful of their weighted-down alpine counterparts, cross country skiers found that telemarking offered them the perfect entree to the slopes—downhill skiing on free-heel equipment. The control and lightness of telemark gear seemed more in keeping with their sport of track skiing. These skiers found out, as well, that their bushwhacking and backcountry skiing could benefit from greater turning skills and the control the telemark turn allows.

In the late 1970s and early 1980s, telemark skiing boomed in popularity throughout the United States. Today, more and more downhill areas accept the telemarker on their slopes, and their instructors (who were among the first to fall for the sport) are teaching downhill nordic technique to beginners and experienced skiers alike. Competitions have sprung up, such as the North American Telemark Championships in Colorado, first held in 1982. Telemark festivals now take place from New England to California, complete with lessons, races, and equipment demonstrations from some of the biggest names in the ski-manufacturing industry. The North American Telemark Organization (NATO) thrives on the enthusiasm of telemark converts. Even somewhat offbeat world records are being established, only to be quickly surpassed by other records. At Mad River Glen in March 1984, for example, 105 nordic skiers linked arms to break the existing group telemark turn world record of 86 skiers set earlier the same month at Breckenridge, Colorado.

But perhaps the finest thing about telemark skiing today is that it completes an historical cycle. For, in the days before chairlifts, before large commercial alpine skiing developments, all skiing was a combination of cross country and downhill. Skiers climbed hills on wide, flexible skis with free-heel bindings then skied down those hills on the same skis. By adopting elements of both, the telemarker takes advantage of lift-served slopes to ski downhill on what are, essentially, cross country skis. Thus, in the best sense, telemark skiing is *complete skiing*, a sport that enjoys modern technology with a refinement of technique and equipment from the days when cross country and downhill were one and the same.

CHAPTER 2

SELECTING EQUIPMENT

Telemark skiing has its own special equipment. Although closely connected to both alpine and nordic gear, the skis, boots, poles, and accoutrements of cross country downhill must perform specific tasks, and thus have special requirements. Interestingly, these requirements resemble those of the past, when all skiing was a combination of cross country and downhill. So for a moment, forget the gladiator boots of downhill, the dancing slippers of cross country racing, and other modern specializations of gear. Just as telemark technique is based on the best of the past, so, too, is modern telemark equipment a refinement of the basic gear of original skiing.

To work well, telemark equipment must be rugged yet lightweight enough to keep you skiing all day long. It should respond readily to your technique, but also be reliably steady when you need more edge, better balance, or a deeper pole plant than you first anticipate. Above all, it must work with you, not against you, as you develop the balance and graceful arc of the telemark turn.

You may think that telemark equipment means nothing more than skis, boots, and poles. Hardware is, of course, crucial. But there is another side, too, and that's software—clothing, eyewear, and accessories that make your day on the slopes a pleasurable one. Both of these categories merit consideration before you go out.

HARDWARE

Financially speaking, hardware will be the biggest commitment you'll make when you decide to take up telemarking. It's astonishing how many people still make their hardware decisions based on little or no knowledge or homework. Don't make that mistake. Racy graphics and high-tech materials may be attractive, but what really counts is performance. If you take the time beforehand to shop around and to consult

9

with friends and experienced professionals before making a choice, you will start your telemark skiing off right.

A word about ski-shop personnel: Many retailers of telemarking equipment are in the business because they love the sport. Likely as not, they will be happy to skip the sales pitch and simply talk with you about your experience and needs. You have a right to expect counsel before, during, and after your purchase, so get it—preferably from several sources. An abrupt purchase may mean an abrupt disappointment on the slopes. Take your time. Good retailers with good equipment know that they benefit from an educated buyer and won't mind working for your business.

With that in mind, let's take a look at what you should consider when purchasing telemark hardware.

SKIS. Skis are the prime ingredient. In the past, telemarking skis were little more than ordinary cross country skis. Today, though, many manufacturers produce skis designed exclusively for telemark skiing. While usually more expensive than regular touring models, these skis address the specific needs of telemarking, and thus merit your fullest consideration.

The materials used in telemarking skis today are almost entirely synthetic. Indeed, the traditional wood skis of the past were on their way out of the American market just as telemarking was becoming a part of the skiing scene here. The reason for this is simple: wood skis, while aesthetically pleasing, don't stand up well to the strain of constant turns. Also, the synthetics tend to be lighter, and so are easier to manage over the long haul. They also require less maintenance than wood, and their bases glide better over all types of snow. From the standpoint of the telemarker, then, synthetic skis are the choice. (Some synthetic skis incorporate wood as a layer, or as the core of the ski, on the theory that this improves a ski's responsiveness. The trend, however, seems to be away from this, as better synthetics are developed.)

Synthetic telemark skis are constructed by one of two methods. The first of these is called sandwich construction. In this method, polyethylene or another synthetic is layered above and below a central core and cemented with epoxy or another strong adhesive. The other method is called torsion-box (or wet-wrap) construction. Here, layers of material are wrapped or fitted around a central core, then pressed and molded. Each method has its partisans. Many believe that sandwich construction can be sturdier. Proponents of the torsion box claim a more torsionally rigid ski is produced this way.

Whatever the construction method used, telemark skis share certain characteristics. These have to do with length, width, shape, and flex. Stiffness and torsional rigidity are also important aspects of telemark skis. Each of these factors relates to you—your height, weight, skill level, and personal tastes. Based on these considerations, here are guidelines to indicate what you should look for in a pair of telemark skis.

Length is the easiest factor to determine. Like other cross country skis, you can figure the length of your telemark skis by the time-honored reach test: Standing with your arm held straight upward, the ski should reach to your wrist. But remember that this is a rule-of-thumb test for regular cross country skis for a person of average weight. For telemarking, you'll want a ski with a softer flex (explained below), so if you err, make it on the side of a shorter (and, thus, softer) ski. Also, if you're heavy for your height, consider a slightly longer ski; if you are light, at least look over slightly shorter skis. A reliable salesperson is important in this matter. If you are uncertain, though, stick with the reach test.

Width and shape go together on telemark skis. Because telemarking involves primarily turning on downhill slopes, your telemark skis should have a good deal of sidecut. Sidecut means that the waist of the ski—where your foot rests—is narrower than the tip or the tail. This hourglass shape aids in turning. Generally, the more pronounced the sidecut, (that is, the greater the difference between the width of the waist and the widths of the tip and tail), the more readily the ski will turn. This can be an advantage, but you don't want too much sidecut or you'll slip into a turn too quickly, with less control.

Look for skis with tips and tails measuring 57 to 65 millimeters across, and a waist in the low to mid-50s. A slightly wider tip than tail is the norm. For example, you could probably find many reliable telemark skis with a sidecut profile of, roughly, 62-54-58 millimeters (tip-waist-tail).

Flex is a crucial element in telemark skis, and it's where they part company dramatically from classic cross country skis. Flex (or camber) is the "bow" underneath your foot. For in-track cross country skiing, a relatively stiff flex (with the bow high, and the center of the ski raised up slightly from the snow) is desirable, because it maximizes the kick-and-glide motion of track skiing. On a telemark ski, however, a stiff flex prevents accurate turning and carving.

This is because when you initiate a telemark turn, the flex actually reverses—the arc of the ski switches from a high center and low tip and tail, to a low center and raised tip and tail. This reverse camber is crucial to the turn; if the bow is high in the center, you cannot get a clean, full-length edge onto the snow for your turn.

Because you will not require much in the way of kick-and-glide on lift-served slopes but will want adequate turning and tracking (tracking is the way a ski follows a line or curve), look for a telemark ski with a relatively soft flex. A word of warning, though: don't settle for a ski that's too soft—it will overturn.

How soft is soft? Experience is the best teacher, but determining the right flex for you shouldn't be an impossible task. A modification of the so-called paper test will tell you if a telemark ski has the right flex. For regular cross country skis, flex is determined this way: Place a slip of paper underneath a pair of skis, right at the center. Then stand with both feet on the center of a pair of skis, where your boots would be. If a friend can just slip the paper out from underneath the skis, they have the right flex for you. Now, modify that test for telemark skis. Since the flex should be softer, your friend shouldn't be able to pull the piece of paper out from under the skis while you stand on them. That's admittedly inexact, and you must be careful not to find skis that are too soft. Still, it is better to err on the side of softer flex than on stiffer flex.

Torsional rigidity is the tendency of a ski to resist twisting along the long axis of the ski. This matters because when you turn, you want your skis to hold their edges onto the snow, without twisting or turning. A torsionally rigid ski performs well on hard-pack snow like that found at downhill areas, avoiding the slipouts of more twisty skis. Combined with adequate sidecut and soft flex, it provides the balance of turning ability and stiffness necessary for good nordic downhill technique.

A word about tips and tails: Both should be stiff. Again, this assumes you will be telemarking on lift-served, packed-snow slopes, free of deep powder. A stiff tip provides holding power on hard pack; softer tips tend to "chatter" along bumps and irregularities (if you are skiing powder, you may want a softer tip; this floats better than a stiffer tip on soft snow). And a stiff tail helps your carving and tracking on packed slopes.

One other aspect of telemark skis sets them apart from most cross country models: metal edges. Like those on alpine skis, the metal edges of telemark skis are crucial to turning. They bite into the snow with sufficient strength for you to carve turns at high rates of speed, and they form the sharp surface necessary for proper tracking during a telemark turn. While virtually all telemark skis have metal edges, there are variations within the group. For example, some skis have edges that are set into the base, flush with the sidewall of the ski. Others have offset metal edges; these protrude a bit from the edge of the sidewall. Choice between the two depends on personal preference, because both are reliable (some claim that offset edges track better, but this, too, seems to depend on whom you talk to). Any metal edge, by the way, should be made of high-quality steel, because this will take and hold a good, sharp edge. Softer metals are rarely acceptable substitutes.

Another variation involves the continuous (or "alpine") metal edge versus the cracked, or segmented, metal edge. A continuous edge, as you might guess, runs in a single piece down the length of the ski. Cracked metal edges look quite similar, but on close inspection, are seen to consist of many small segments, carefully lined up along the edges of the ski. The different edges have different purposes. The cracked edge is

designed for greater control in backcountry and mountaineering situations. For the telemark skier on lift-served slopes, though, the continuous edge is preferred. It gives greater control on packed slopes and bites better on harder snows.

In summary, a good telemark ski incorporates features designed specifically for telemark technique on lift-served slopes: torsional rigidity, a stiff tip and tail, soft flex (or camber), pronounced sidecut, and continuous edges.

BOOTS. Next to skis, good telemark boots are your most important consideration. Not only are they necessary for control, they are crucial to comfort. Wet, cold, uncomfortable feet are the most common complaints among new telemarkers; they can cut short any ski outing. So, before you consider any other feature of a boot, remember: they must fit well, be waterproof, and keep your feet warm throughout the day.

After those requirements, the next quality a telemark boot must have is torsional rigidity. As with a ski, this means that it will resist twisting from side to side along its long (that is, front-to-back) axis. The reason for this is straightforward: When you perform the telemark turn, a lot of force is directed to the right or left, depending on your direction. If a free-heel boot doesn't resist this force, your heel tends to slip off the ski, ruining your turn.

Because the turn relies so much on control, your boots must deliver that control from your legs to your skis without twisting off to the side. When shopping for boots, then, be sure to test this quality. Twist the sole of the boots as hard as you can to the left and right. A good boot will give very little in either direction.

At the same time, a telemark boot should bend fairly easily in an up-and-down direction. Think of it: When you telemark, your boot is snapped into a toe binding. To execute the turn, you drop one knee down, raising the heel of that boot. A boot whose sole won't raise easily from the ski may make the maneuver more difficult than it should be. It is this combination—high torsional rigidity combined with good up-and-down flex—that sets a high-quality telemark boot apart from its low-quality brethren.

Boot quality depends upon materials and construction methods. Leather is still the favored material for telemark-boot uppers. It is supple, long-lasting, and can be waterproofed easily. It is also rather expensive, especially in the full-grain models (full-grain leather includes the inner and exterior layers of hide; split-grain leather consists only of an inner layer of hide). Some split-grain models are perfectly sufficient for telemarking, but let the buyer beware. If you can afford full-grain, and feel committed enough to the sport to want a boot that will last many years, look to these models for your choice.

Almost everywhere today, sole material consists of Vibram, and for good reason. The stuff has proven itself. You should note the thickness of the sole of your prospective boots and see that it matches your bindings (this is explained fully below). Or better yet, buy your boots first, then match a binding to them. The variance of sole thickness will affect the up-and-down flex of your boot, too, as well as its warmth; some boots also have baffled soles, in which dead air is trapped for added warmth underfoot. Since warmth and flex are largely a matter of personal taste, check out several thicknesses, if possible.

The width of a boot's toepiece, where it mates to the binding, is in most cases the standard, 75-millimeter, three-pin version, known as the nordic norm. In recent years, much has been made of the new, so-called boot-binding systems. For now, though, these are manufactured primarily for the in-track and touring skier. The boot-binding systems have yet to prove themselves in the telemark world, especially in terms of torsional rigidity. It may be that one day boot-binding systems will replace the 75-millimeter for telemarking. That day, though, has not yet come. Stick with the nordic norm.

Some soles now incorporate steel plates underneath or inside the toepiece. Others have steel reinforcements for the binding-pin holes. Nylon or steel shanks under the ball of the foot may also be incorporated into a boot; the nylon gives good flex, while steel increases the strength and torsional rigidity. These reinforcements and inserts add weight and cost to a boot, but also increase the life and durability of a good model. The choice is yours to make.

One other material consideration is the lace material of a boot. While most telemark boots use standard laces, at least one model is now being manufactured with Velcro straps (from the Merrell Boot Company). Velcro straps allow you to close each strap with infinite adjustment—resulting in comfort and "customized" fit.

The method by which a boot is constructed matters for two reasons: comfort and durability. The comfort factor is highly personal, and so individual testing is necessary. You may want to consider, though, that many boots are now made on American lasts, as opposed to European lasts. European models tend to be narrower, while American models are wider and sometimes rounder in the toe box. To choose between the two, try a model of each at the same time. Most Americans tend to find the American last more comfortable, but still, check first: You may have European feet.

Boot welts are important in terms of durability and waterproofness. The welt is the area between a boot's sole and upper through which they are stitched together. The so-called Norwegian welt is the most elaborate and reliable of stitching methods, but it adds cost. Other welts will need more care and attention for waterproofing. Also important for waterproof qualities is the gusseted tongue; that is, a boot tongue that's

15

attached to the rest of the upper by triangular gussets running the length of the tongue. See to it that your boot has them.

Linings for boots come in many shapes and sizes. Fleece lining is traditional, but seems to be losing ground to good leather liners and various insulating materials—foams and other air-trapping materials. Remember that on lift-served slopes, you'll be spending lots of time dangling in the air, inactive. You'll want the extra warmth that a good liner provides.

One of the most dramatic developments in recent years has been the advent of double boots. This is actually an old idea that's been revived in the public imagination by several top-quality models. These are boots with a thinner inner boot that mates to a sturdy outer boot. They offer a distinct advantage in both comfort and control and are especially popular in the wet-snow regions of the American West for their durability and waterproofness. They are also very expensive, sometimes twice as expensive as regular telemark boots. Owners swear by them, though, so if you're willing to pay for the best, you should try on a few models.

Finally, you will notice when shopping for boots that there are several different heights from which to choose. The classic, ankle-high telemark boot offers sufficient support and control for most beginners, but taller boots are now available—some reaching up to the middle of the calf. The strength of your technique—and your ankles—is important here. The taller models may be attractive to you, but keep in mind that they mean more weight on your feet, and possibly more fatigue as a result. One modest indication of which height to choose is based on your past skiing experience. If you've been a downhill skier all your life, the extra weight and height may not make any difference to you; indeed, it may be an advantage. If, on the other hand, you're taking up telemark skiing from a background as a cross country track skier, you may prefer the lighter weight that an ankle-high boot provides. And don't worry that a smaller boot won't last as long; quality of materials and construction are what's important, not simply size.

BINDINGS. The critical connection between skier and ski comes at the point where binding meets boot. As noted above, your bindings should match your boots in width. In most cases, this means the standard three-pin, 75-millimeter-wide nordic norm. Seventy-one millimeter, 79-millimeter, and other widths are available, but their advantage is hard to discern in terms of telemark skiing. Look to the 75-millimeter models for your choice.

Both plastic and metal bindings are available to telemark skiers, but most skiers prefer metal. Plastics like Delrin are tough and lightweight, but may snap or crack with extended use. A better choice for telemark skiers is metal, and of these, high-quality aluminum probably offers the best compromise between weight and durability. Aluminum telemark bindings are also widely available from many manufacturers with high quality standards, and so they are a safe bet across the board.

A binding's bail, the part of the binding that fits over the boot's toe-piece and clamps down, comes in flat and round versions. While each is good, some telemarkers prefer the flat bail for extra holding power. The tradeoff is that a flat bail may wear on a boot more readily than a round version. To correct this, some bails come with nylon coatings that protect the leather and sole of the boot.

When choosing a binding, check both hinges of the bail carefully. It's here that most bails eventually come apart. A good hinge will have a solid connection between bail and sidewall of the binding, sometimes using a heavier metal, such as steel, for the rotation pin.

Other parts of a binding include the latch for the bail, anchoring screws, and a heelplate. In most cases, the latch should be adjustable. This allows you to fix the bail over the boot's toepiece at one of several degrees of tension. If you're comfortable with the tension offered by a single-latch binding, fine; otherwise, spend the extra dollar or two for an adjustable one (some bindings are also available with two interchangeable bails of different heights for different sole thicknesses).

17

The anchoring screws of a binding do just that—anchor the binding on the ski. Posi-drive screws are the industry norm, and they are quite reliable. Mounting your bindings onto your skis, by the way, must be done correctly or you'll lose your skis in short order. If you don't know how to mount your bindings, let a professional do it.

Heelplates of bindings come in many shapes and sizes. All are reliable. Some skiers like heelplates with metal teeth that stick up for added purchase on the boot sole. Others believe this wears the sole unduly. If you have chosen your boots carefully, though, you shouldn't have much trouble with purchase, because the boots won't slip from side to side.

Recently, telemark bindings have appeared that include a thick strip of heavy-duty plastic running from the toe of the binding down to the heel, fitting underneath the boot and attaching to the heel. These models practically guarantee lateral stability, and the manufacturers—among them Alpine Research and Marker—are known for their quality construction. They add weight, however, and seem to be intended more for backcountry and mountaineering use than for lift-served telemarking. They are also very expensive; some start at $130 and go up from there, depending on specific features.

Sometimes telemarkers include heel locators as part of their binding arrangement. Heel locators consist of a V-shaped piece of plastic mounted vertically on the ski, just behind the boot heel, and an elongated piece of plastic mounted on the heel itself. When you bring your heel down on the ski, the reasoning goes, the heel piece fits into the notch of the V, centering your boot on the ski and preventing side-to-side motion. While many telemarkers and backcountry enthusiasts recommend them, others find them an annoyance, and still others call them dangerous. Further, heel locators only duplicate the lateral stability you'll get from a well-made telemark boot. If you are considering buying them, rent a pair of telemark skis with heel locators first and see if you like skiing on them.

There's one other piece of binding equipment you must have—a safety strap. Lift-served areas simply won't allow you on the slopes without them, for good reason: A runaway ski is dangerous. Find a good, sturdy pair—nylon is an excellent material—and make sure that they will attach reliably to both your boots and bindings. Don't be afraid to make the strap shorter if necessary. Sometimes a strap that is too long will create a loop that the tip of your trailing ski will get caught in. Mount the safety strap so that its loop is to the outside.

POLES. The last, but by no means least, of the basic tools you'll need for telemark skiing are poles. Like bindings, they represent a fairly easy choice of equipment.

Poles are used for balance and for planting in the snow, so they've got to be sturdy yet relatively light. Cross country poles usually come in one of three materials: tonkin (or bamboo), fiberglass, and aluminum alloy. Of these, tonkin is considered unacceptable for telemarking. It just isn't sturdy enough. Fiberglass is far better, although cheaper models can be too brittle under heavy stress. Fiberglass is lightweight, though, and comes in some very rugged versions. If you select fiberglass, be sure to consider poles with a fiberglass-epoxy blend in the shaft. These are more durable than other models.

Of all shaft materials, aluminum is by far the sturdiest, and the most widely available, in poles that are built specifically for telemark skiing. This is for good reason. Aluminum is lightweight, versatile, and quite adaptable to the stresses and strains of nordic downhill. The prices of aluminum poles are higher, but they are worth the investment in terms of the lifetime of the product.

Pole grips come in all shapes and sizes. Backcountry skiers and many telemarkers like pistol grips, although they are by no means necessary (these are grips having ridges that fit between your fingers). Other grips include the simple rounded grip and oval grips with a ridge running down the length of the grip's front. High-quality leather grips, especially the suede versions, are easy to grasp; plastic grips are durable, if sometimes slippery. In any case, make sure your grip has an adjustable strap, so you can adjust it to fit your hand. Nylon straps are durable but sometimes less comfortable than leather straps.

The sizes and shapes of pole baskets are now legion, but for telemark skiing, it's good to stick to basics. A simple round plastic basket, fairly large, is a safe bet. Some oval or asymmetrical baskets have their fans, too, because there's less basket pushing down into the snow as you remove your pole from it. To choose, think of the type of skiing you'll be doing. On groomed slopes, a large, powder-type basket is unnecessary— you won't need that much flotation. In softer snow or deep powder, a large, round powder basket should be your choice.

Almost all pole tips—the part that digs into the snow—are now made of top-quality carbide steel to stand up to the punishment incurred during thousands of pole plants. Your pole tip, it should be noted, should point forward at the very end. This makes it easier to remove from the snow as you withdraw your pole from the snow.

Finally, there is the question of pole length. Much has been made lately of the claim that telemark poles should be shorter than regular cross country poles. The reasoning is that they will be easier to use when you're in downhill motion. The jury still seems to be out on this one, though. For now, stick with the traditional method of determining the proper length of pole for you: Stand on the floor in your stocking feet. The top of the pole's handle should just reach your armpit. If you think you'd prefer a shorter pole, try one that's five centimeters shorter.

SOFTWARE

Back in the days when all skiing was essentially a combination of downhill and cross country, there was very little specialized ski clothing available. Like skis, boots, bindings, and poles, ski clothing was generalized, relatively undeveloped. Then came the downhill craze of the 1950s and 1960s. Suddenly, specialized downhill clothing was everywhere: snow suits, stretch pants, and a cornucopia of colorful fashions. Cross country skiers and three-pin downhillers, however, stayed a pretty rustic lot, tucking bluejeans into kneesocks, wearing wool and down parkas, and only occasionally—such as with knickers—making a concession to practicality.

Then in the late 1970s, cross country clothing underwent its own revolution. Practical, attractive clothing appeared for the track skier and nordic downhiller. Woolly knickers were refined to allow more freedom of movement. High-tech, useful synthetics, such as polypropylene and Gore-Tex, gained widespread acceptance. Better cuts of clothing, combined with proper venting and layering, provided skiers with maximum comfort and durability. What's more, skiers began to discover that their software could be not only practical, but downright attractive as well.

Of course, the telemark skier has different needs from either the track skier or the diehard downhiller. As you might expect, the ideal clothing for a telemarker follows the same pattern as the hardware: It combines the best of both track-ski togs and downhill duds. Personal experimentation taught even the most rustic telemarker that the new clothing, and the new ideas about what ski clothing should do, made for a more comfortable, enjoyable day on the slopes.

Telemark clothing must perform two functions at once. First, it must be warm enough to keep you from freezing while on the lifts. Second, it must not be too warm, or you'll overheat when exercising. It must also be easily removed and put back on, so you can adjust to the pace of the day.

To achieve this balance, telemark skiers in increasing numbers have adopted the layering system of clothing from track skiers. The layering system consists of three layers of clothing, each adapted to a specific function: an inner layer for comfort against the skin, a middle layer for insulation and warmth, and an outer layer for protection against wind, water, and other vagaries of nature. There are other details to consider, too, but for now, let's look at the basics of the layering system.

INNER LAYER. Your inner layer rests next to your skin, and so comfort is of prime importance. Because telemark skiing involves lots of exercise combined with periods of inactivity, your body tends to perspire, then cool off. To avoid a chill, you should have an inner layer that

wicks this moisture away from your skin, leaving it dry and comfortable.

For this purpose, most day-to-day inner layers are unacceptable. Cotton, for example, gets wet and stays that way. Wool will stay warm when wet, but this can be quite scratchy and uncomfortable. Cotton-wool blends are only marginally better; their purpose is to make wool feel better, but they still don't solve the problem of that unpleasant, soggy sensation. Silk underwear offers a better choice, and its feel is delicious. Yet like the others, its wicking properties leave something to be desired.

A relatively new synthetic, polypropylene, is the preferred inner layer among telemarkers and track skiers alike. The reason is straightforward: It simply wicks away moisture better than any other fabric widely available. It keeps your skin dry, and thus prevents cooling due to contact with moisture. The first garments made of polypropylene tended to feel a bit like plastic on the skin, but that problem has been largely solved by better weaves and lighter polypropylene fabric. A better inner layer hasn't yet been invented.

When you shop for polypropylene underwear, be sure to find both tops and bottoms. Expect to pay more than you would for regular longjohns, but expect the price to be worth the payback in comfort. And remember, to work well the stuff has to rest against your skin; if you wear it over cotton briefs or other underwear, you'll stay cold and clammy in those areas.

MIDDLE LAYER. This is your insulating and absorbing layer, and here you'll find many choices of high-quality clothing. There's one consideration to keep in mind: When your inner layer wicks away moisture from your skin, it deposits it here, inside your middle layer. Hence, you'll want to use a material that stays warm when wet. Telemarkers rarely perspire as much as cross country track skiers, but wetness is still a factor in comfort. For that reason again, cotton is out. So is down: It doesn't insulate well when wet and has the extra disadvantage of being too warm when dry. A wool sweater, though, is fine, as are garments made of other materials—such polyester weaves, for example, as pile and bunting. If you choose wool, adjust your choice of thickness to how cold you usually get in the out-of-doors. Many telemarkers find that a thin, loose wool weave, in combination with a windproof outer layer, keeps them warm enough in periods between downhill runs. Others prefer a heavy wool sweater, perhaps because they don't exert themselves as much when telemarking. If you like pile, on the other hand, you won't have to worry as much about moisture, since pile absorbs very little (the moisture stays between your inner and middle layers). Some piles have fleece inner layers, and this adds warmth by trapping air close to your body.

Your middle layer should also protect your neck and lower regions. For your neck, a wool-nylon turtleneck or even a dickey will be comfortable. A turtleneck also traps warmed air that would otherwise escape quickly. For your legs, a layer of wool underwear works well in combination with a polypropylene inner layer. Choose a pair that is comfortable yet traps a bit of air for extra warmth. Wool pants or wool knickers are still the most popular choice for a middle-and-outer layer for the legs.

Because telemark skiing involves lots of bending and stretching for your legs, most skiers seem to prefer a wool knicker and long stocking combination over long pants. Bib knickers, which protect your front and back torso as well as your legs, are also popular. Finally, there are now some cotton knickers, especially corduroy, that have been chemically treated for water repellency, and these are perfectly fine for the average telemark skier.

Remember that your middle layer doesn't have to consist of just one garment. Indeed, several layers of clothing may be an advantage, considering the stop-and-go pace of telemark skiing. When you reach the liftline, you can put on an extra layer of insulation, then remove it when you're skiing. Also, several thin layers trap air warmed by your body better than one thick layer. With two or more middle layers, you can adjust your clothing to suit the pace of the day.

OUTER LAYER. Your outer layer forms a protective barrier between you and the elements. To work well, it must protect from wind and water yet have sufficient venting to prevent you from overheating on the slopes. Venting is secondary, though, for the telemarker, because most of the time he's rushing down the slope with wind and possibly snow facing him. So if you must choose between the two, look to protection.

Ski-clothing manufacturers now produce outer layers with plenty of room in the shoulders, arms, and chest. This is critical for the telemark skier, who needs room to move in these areas. Also important are zip fronts, either half-length (anoraks) or full-length in the torso, for venting and easy adjustment of layers.

The classic windproof and waterproof shell is an ideal outer layer for telemark skiing. It affords protection but is light and flexible. Materials used include nylon and other synthetics. Some shells now come with "pitzips" and other zippers that allow venting while keeping your front protected—these extra vents are highly recommended. Other shells are constructed of Gore-Tex, Klimate, or other synthetics that breathe when you wear them. They combine this breatheability with waterproof, windproof qualities and have proven themselves in conditions ranging from afternoons on the slopes to months in the backcountry. While costly, these can provide the ultimate in outer-layer comfort and are generally worth the cost. Whatever the material, make sure that your shell has a hood and drawstrings or elastic in the waist and cuffs.

Some outer layers now sport ultrathin insulating materials such as Thinsulate, PolarGuard, Hollofil, Quallofil, and others. Again, these are expensive, but they do the job of down with less bulk. Further, they stay warm when wet. Combined with a waterproof, breatheable outer shell, they are the last word in outdoor gear. A question, though, arises as to whether these don't amount to overkill for the active telemarker. They can often be too warm when you're exercising. Again, personal preference dominates here. If you tend to become cold easily, consider these as extra insulation to your middle layer. Otherwise, stick to several middle layers and concentrate on windproofing and waterproofing for your outer-layer requirements.

These are the basic ingredients of the layering system, but software requirements don't end here. To be fully equipped for nordic downhill, you'll need headgear, gloves, and other accessories. Here are a few thoughts on some of the software trimmings.

HATS, GLOVES, ET AL. Since heat escapes from your head faster than any other part of your body, you should have a good cap for telemarking. Knit wool caps, like those made for alpine skiers, are a good choice for the telemarker. If, on the other hand, you plan to exert yourself quite a bit—say, by racing up hills you've just telemarked down for an extra thrill—a full alpine cap will be too warm. A good compromise between the two would be a light knit wool cap or a cap in a wool-nylon blend. Some caps have a special inner sweatband, too, and these are recommended for vigorous telemarkers. If you ski in the late season, though, consider carrying along a billed cap, like a baseball cap. Late-winter and spring skiing may require the protection from sunshine and snow glare that a baseball cap affords.

Good gloves will go a long way toward insuring that you'll stay warm and comfortable on the slopes. Usually, a glove must provide insulation, wicking, and outer-layer protection all in one unit. Fortunately, many gloves are now being offered with polypropylene inners, layers of high-tech, superthin insulation, and synthetic outer shells. Since water repellency and breatheability are crucial to the proper functioning of a glove, the outer shell should be either of Gore-Tex or another similar breatheable material or a chemically treated nylon layer. Check to see that a glove fits correctly and gives you sufficient dexterity to handle your ski poles and other gear. Mittens are warmer than gloves, by the way, but you'll sacrifice some freedom of movement. If you like mittens, get a good pair of woolen ones and a pair of nylon shells with leather palms that fit over them. This will make your hand gear more adjustable to changing conditions.

Gaiters aren't particularly necessary on groomed slopes, but they are useful when you're skiing deeper snow or wet, heavy snow. Gaiters are leggings that fit over your boots and lower legs and are designed to keep

out snow and water. They come in ankle-high, mid-calf, and knee-high sizes. Try to find a pair that features sturdy loops underfoot (to keep them in place) and a good, tight cuff. While some gaiters are insulated, a simple, one-layer pair should suffice for the lift-served telemark skier.

Socks, of course, are your main source of insulation in a part of the body particularly susceptible to cold—your feet. Wool socks are toasty warm, perfect for the telemarker. If you plan to be very active, include a pair of polypropylene or silk socks to wear under your wool ones. These will wick away moisture and keep your feet comfortable.

Other small items include sunscreen and sunglasses. The amount of glare on downhill slopes is tremendous, especially in the late winter and spring. Find sunglasses that hook around your ears and use a piece of string or special sports strap to keep them on in case you take a tumble. Side flaps, such as those found on glacier glasses, are useful but not critical unless the sun is very bright (due to spring skiing or high altitude) or you expect long exposure. For sunscreen, use any high-protection formula. Some have ratings marked on their containers. Moderately protective screens have a rating of about nine, while higher ratings offer greater protection. If your skin is very sensitive, or the sun is especially strong, you can use a full sun block, such as zinc oxide, but this is probably overkill. Glycerin or lanolin-based sunscreens also offer some wind protection.

Finally, you may want to use a fanny pack or similar pack. This can be very useful on the slopes, to carry sunscreen, waxes, spare parts (such as binding bails), snacks, and to store your extra clothing as you warm up or cool down. Look for a pack with a full-length, heavy-duty zipper, a reliable closure, and compartments to separate your waxes and suncreen from your clothing and lunch.

CHAPTER 3

TELEMARK TECHNIQUE

Think his chapter deals with learning the telemark turn. It takes you from the beginning stages through advanced techniques, and is divided into eight separate lessons. The concept behind our approach is to teach one thing at a time in order to build a foundation of one skill upon another. The lessons are designed to help you understand both *how* to make a telemark turn and *why* the skis behave as they do on the snow.

The first five lessons concentrate on specific components of the telemark turn; mastering the techniques in one lesson enables you to go on to the next. We recommend staying with each lesson, practicing the exercise it demonstrates, until you feel comfortable and in control. Then go on to the next lesson. Have realistic expectations and do not be disappointed if you aren't sweeping down the slopes in perfectly executed telemark turns on your first or second outing. Try to focus on the specific exercises in each lesson rather than rushing the process before you're ready to move on.

In Lesson 6, which deals with linking turns, you will need to rely on all your newly developed skills to link turns down a slope, negotiating it from top to bottom with correct telemark technique. In essence, this is the lesson that brings it all together. Lessons 7 and 8 are for the advanced skier. These deal with adjusting your technique to handle steep slopes and moguled slopes. They do not, however, call upon any skills other than those covered in preceding lessons. But when you're at the point where you are skiing down steep slopes or moguled fields, the telemark turn itself should be already mastered and you should be able to ski with a certain degree of self-expression that comes from experience, not wholly from a book.

Before moving onto the first lesson, we have a few words about snow conditions and skiing at lift-served slopes on nordic skis.

The lessons in this chapter are designed to be practiced on packed-powder slopes or in shallow powder—either open fields that you may know of or slopes at a lift-served ski area. Deep powder makes it difficult to learn the telemark turn, for it adds an extra dimension to the dynamics of the turn—resistance from deep snow. Skiing in powder eight inches deep and deeper is a skill to be developed once you have mastered the telemark in more favorable learning conditions. Likewise, when there is little or no "give" to the snow—as on ice or very fast corn snow—it is difficult to set your ski edges and therefore these conditions are also an obstacle to learning.

When skiing at a lift-served ski area, bear in mind the following points. First and foremost, some areas do not allow nordic skis to be used on their trails. This is, however, changing rapidly, and if you are in ski country one area is surely going to allow nordic gear if another does not. But to be on the safe side, always check ahead, and it is best for the acceptance of telemarking as a regular part of ski-area life if you respect no-nordic rules where they exist.

If you intend to ride lifts, remember that your free-heel binding makes getting on a chairlift a little different than getting on with fixed-heel alpine gear. However, your skis will not dangle dangerously if you remember simply to lift your knees as the chair lifts you off the ground. Nordic skis are traditionally lighter than alpine skis, and you can position them on the ski rest easily once airborne. When descending a slope, respect the ski area's trails; even though you have cross country skis it doesn't mean you can ski off into land an area has designated closed to skiing. You will also need a safety strap at a lift-served area. Chapter 2 tells how to obtain a safety strap if you don't have one.

Finally, remember that telemark technique requires typically wider turns and a slower overall speed while descending a slope than standard alpine parallel or stem-christy technique. This means that most of the skiers at an alpine ski area are going to be traveling in a different path at a different speed than you will be traveling while telemarking. In other words, don't get run over from behind because you're traveling slower and don't turn out into another skier's path. Since telemarking requires a degree of soft surface snow in which to set an edge, sometimes the best bet is to stick to the sides of trails where there is frequently a skied-off build-up of surface snow.

LESSON 1
TELEMARK POSITION

The telemark turn is predicated on weight and angulation. The characteristic stance shown here is both elegant and practical. The position of the knees helps absorb shock and maintain balance. If you look closely at this photo, you will be able to see how the entire body position itself, from ankles through arms, uses weight and angulation to absorb shock and maintain balance. In this photo, you can almost feel the skier sweeping through the turn . . .

This photo is our ideal, our paradigm. In the pages that follow, the telemark turn will be broken down into its separate elements, but remember these elements come together in a single smooth motion: the telemark turn.

Lesson 1 acquaints you with the fundamental telemark position. It can be practiced on flat ground or a slight incline. We are striving in this first lesson to help you feel at ease in the telemark position and to make a key point: The telemark turn is actually nothing more than an extension of the diagonal stride—the fundamental kick and glide—of cross country skiing.

In this first lesson, don't worry about turning, *per se*. Actually, you will not be traveling fast enough to allow a telemark turn. Concentrate on acquainting yourself with your skis and the telemark position.

1. Begin by striding across an open field with a slight incline. Use your normal, comfortable diagonal stride and ski straight down the slope. You don't have to be going fast; you just need enough momentum to see what it feels like to glide in the telemark position. We are not going to be turning in this lesson; just open-field skiing to introduce the telemark position to you.

2. With arms held out, bent slightly at the elbows as shown, slide one knee forward. Spread your feet slightly, and bend your knees to lower your torso. Keep skis flat on the snow; the tip of the trailing ski should be just ahead of your forward boot. Think of sliding the one ski forward as a natural extension of the diagonal stride.

32

3. Here is a side view of what you are trying to do. The bent knees and slightly split stance deliver control and stability. Knees are bent at about a 90-degree angle; note that the skier's right knee is just above his left ankle and that he is bent only slightly forward at the waist.

4. Now, stand back up. Remember the shock-absorbing nature of the telemark position. As you stand up, slide the opposite knee forward. Think about making a smooth transition from the position in the previous photo to an upright position to sliding the opposite knee forward. Once again, the motion is fundamentally the same as diagonal striding.

5. *Bend both knees again. You are duplicating the position you just practiced, only the opposite knee is forward. Continue practicing this stance and transferring weight while traveling in a straight line down a slight incline. Don't worry about turning here, just worry about getting the feel of the telemark position. Once you can go from one ski to the other smoothly and with balance, you are ready to move onto the next lesson, which is on traversing.*

LESSON 2
THE TRAVERSE

Traversing is a simple and effective way to introduce two further, key elements of the telemark turn: angulation and edging. This photo shows the skier making a simple traverse, but in addition to what we covered in the first lesson, note that he has "rolled" his knees into the hill (angulation) and transferred weight forward over the downhill ski (edging). Result? A wide, gentle turn. Note the long arc of the skier's track across the slope.

Practice traversing on a hill that is too steep to go straight down comfortably but not so steep as to challenge you. As you complete the traverse in either direction, let the arc of the turn take you into a skidding stop. This lesson is not designed to teach you how to link turns; instead, it is designed to give you a feel for edging and angulation. As in Lesson 1, the slope is so slight that it won't allow you to build up enough speed to make a full telemark turn properly. Concentrate on gaining a feel for edging and angulation in Lesson 2.

1. *Begin the traverse at the edge of the slope, giving yourself plenty of room to carve a wide arc across the slope. You are going to ski across the slope, not straight down it as in the previous lesson. Use a diagonal stride or a couple of strong double poles to build up a little momentum, then slide the downhill knee forward (as you practiced in the previous lesson.)*

2. *As you assume the telemark position, roll your forward (downhill) knee into the slope. Note that this results in weight transfer in the upper body, illustrated here by the skier's right shoulder mimicking the rolling of the left knee— which is another example of the close relationship between the telemark turn and the diagonal stride. The rear ski is only slightly weighted.*

3. In this photo, the skier rides the traverse he began in the previous photo through to a skidding stop. We aren't concerned with linking traverses back and forth across the slope; rather, you should traverse through to a stop in one direction and then in the other to negotiate the hill from top to bottom. The key here is to familiarize yourself with the elements of weight transfer (edging) and angulation (rolling the knees). Practice traversing in both directions until you feel comfortably in control. Experiment with rolling the knees to create various degrees of edging power as you traverse and slide to a stop; this teaches you edge control. Also experiment with setting the edge (rolling your knees in) and then releasing it by transferring weight equally onto both skis so the skis ride flat on the snow; this will further develop edge control.

LESSON 3
STEP INITIATION

In the first two lessons, as noted, you were not traveling fast enough to complete a full telemark turn. But having become familiar with the telemark position, edging, and angulation, you are now ready to add a new component that will allow you to ski steeper, faster slopes: step initiation. This and the following three lessons can be practiced on a slope with a pitch similar to that found on the ski-school or beginnner's slope at a lift-served ski area.

However, we are not ready yet to move into linking turns together. In this lesson you'll be making a full telemark turn in one direction, riding it through to a stop, then practicing the same thing in the other direction. Here, we are trying to single out a key component—step initation—for you to practice.

Step initiation, as this photo shows, can be thought of as a bold commitment by the skier to make a turn. The downhill ski is unweighted and placed across the line of travel before the skier transfers his weight onto it. Note something else new in this photo: The skier is using his poles, which have been pretty much window-dressing in the first two lessons.

Before practicing step initiation, take a few runs down the hill using the traversing method you practiced in Lesson 2. This will acquaint you with the greater speed you'll encounter; this speed is needed to practice step initiation.

Perhaps more than any other component of the telemark turn, step initiation relies on diagonal-stride timing. You are stepping up and out and transferring weight from one ski to another.

1. Step initiation begins by unweighting the uphill ski. Simply pick it up off the snow. Once unweighted, you will place it across the line of travel. When replaced on the snow it should be at about a 20- to 30-degree angle to the other ski. This angle may vary according to the tightness of the turn you want to make, but for this lesson, use a 20- to 30-degree angle.

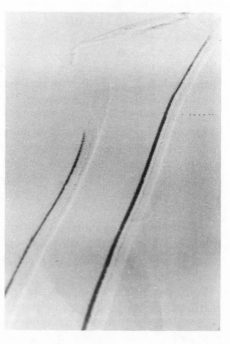

2. Again, as the skier's tracks illustrate, step initiation means picking a ski up off the snow and placing it on edge across the line of travel. Note the straight path of the weighted ski during the step initiation; it does not turn until the edged uphill ski "tells" it to. Note also the angle at which the left-hand ski was replaced on the snow.

3. *Just prior to unweighting the uphill ski, the skier will plant his right pole. The pole plant should be made just ahead of the skier's downhill (right) boot, and out a comfortable distance to the side. In this photo the skier steps up . . .*

4. . . . and here he steps out, setting the ski forward and on its edge. The pole is planted, knees are rolled in . . .

5. . . . and the result is a telemark turn. Ride this turn out to a stop in one direction across the slope, then practice in the other until the step initiation is a smooth, single movement: Plant the pole, unweight the uphill ski, step out, place the ski on edge across your line of travel, roll your knees in, and ride through to a stop in the full telemark position.

LESSON 4
THE SWEEPING TURN

The sweeping turn is the combination of step initiation and follow-through in a stable, full telemark position that allows moving into linking turns. The sweeping telemark turn allows us to introduce a new element: rear ski control. This photo shows how rear ski control is critical to overall control when telemark skiing. The placement and weighting of the rear ski combines with the placement of the forward ski to create, in a sense, a single ski that sweeps through the turn.

The rear ski must be slightly weighted so it will track behind the forward ski and provide control. Each ski in this photo is on edge.

In this lesson, we'll take you from beginning to unweight one ski for step initiation through a full turn and preparing to link this turn with another turn across the slope in the other direction. We are concentrating here on coordinating front and rear skis for the full control that proper telemarking requires.

43

1. In this photo the skier is beginning to unweight his left ski by rolling knees into the slope and shifting weight slightly forward. He is about to make a pole plant.

2. Now, the ski is unweighted, and the skier is stepping into the turn, about to place his left ski across the path of travel of his right ski.

3. The front ski has been placed and weighted across the path of travel. Knees roll into the slope, and the skier begins to redistribute some of his weight to the rear ski in order to keep it tracking and adding control through the turn.

4. Here, knees have been rolled in and the skier has dropped into a full, stable telemark position that he will ride through the turn. Note that now both skis are carving with their edges and that when the knees are rolled in the heels follow, too, naturally rolling into the turn. The proper weight distribution is 70 percent on leading ski and 30 percent on trailing ski. The skier will ride this through the turn until he is ready to stand up and initiate a new turn in the other direction.

LESSON 5
ADDING POWER

In the preceding four lessons we have taken you through the fundamentals of the telemark technique. This and the following lessons refine what you've learned to enhance your technique and allow you to handle a variety of terrains and to link turns down a slope. Lesson 5 deals with adding power to your turn. In many instances, you will want to narrow the radius of your sweeping turns to create greater control. To do this you must impart more power into the act of turning to handle the higher speed and shorter radius of your turn.

Power, however, does not mean muscling or forcing your way through a turn. It refers to timing: force application at specific moments in your turn. Telemark skiing is working *with* the snow and terrain, not forcing your way through it.

Even though this photo shows a lot of power between the skis and the snow, note that the skier has his knees rolled in and he is dropping into the full telemark position. This puts the skis on edge and will lead him into a position in which he can distribute weight properly between front and rear ski as demonstrated in the previous lesson. He is actually working with the snow and the slope, not forcing his way through the turn.

47

1. Begin your turn with a pole plant and by unweighting the uphill ski. Pick the ski up, step forward with it, and place it across your line of travel.

2. Commit your body weight to the forward ski by rolling the forward knee into the hill and unweighting the rear ski. This is the point at which power is added, and it is done by exaggerating angulation and ski edging. This results in greater weight commitment than when you were learning the step initiation.

3. As you ride through the turn, redistribute your weight so that the rear ski is bearing about 30 percent of it. This imparts control and places you in a position to move into a turn across the slope in the other direction. But for the purposes of this lesson, ride the turn out to a skidding stop, then practice in the other direction. Power has brought you through the turn without sacrificing the speed that allows you to link this turn with a new one. Lesson 6, which follows, deals with linking turns, and in linking turns what we've learned in this lesson—speed of initiation—is what sets the pace.

LESSON 6
LINKING TURNS

Linking turns brings all the telemark skills you've learned thus
far together in a smooth journey
from the top to the bottom of a
slope. In essence, linking turns
means going from the solid telemark position learned in Lesson
1 into a turn and then back again
into the telemark position. If you
watch a skilled telemarker come
down a slope, you see that he
goes up and down, alternately
bending his knees and straight-
ening up as he comes in and out
of turns.

The photo here demonstrates a moment of full unweighting on both
skis, essential to making the link between turns. The skier has completed a turn, dropped into and followed through in the telemark position,
and here he is coming up again to begin a new turn. It is critical that
you understand a series of turns includes a smooth transition from
weight commitment through unweighting and into weight commitment again. Again, think of telemark turning as a downhill interpeta-
tion of the fundamental diagonal stride of cross country skiing on the
flats.

1. Keeping your knees bent while crossing the slope, plant your pole and prepare to unweight both skis.

2. Here you stand up, reaching a moment of complete unweighting on your skis. In the photo, the skier's left leg is being slid forward, and knees are beginning to be rolled into the slope. The unweighting shown here, remember, is not a static thing, it is a moment captured photographically while the skier is simultaneously moving his left knee and leg forward for step initiation.

3. *The turning ski is placed forward, across the line of travel, and set on edge to initiate the turn. Rear ski is momentarily unweighted.*

4. Weight is redistributed to the rear ski so that the weight distribution overall is 70 percent front ski, 30 percent rear ski. The skier drops into a stable telemark position.

5. The skier rides out the turn with weight still distributed 70-30 on his skis. Both skis are edged, and the rear ski aids in control by tracking behind the front ski.

6. As the skier begins the next turn, the skis return to a flat (unedged) position on the snow, and unweighting begins. The pole is about to be planted, and this time the right ski is moving forward.

55

7. Weight is transferred onto the turning ski, placing it on edge, and the rear ski is fully unweighted, about to be brought in alongside the forward ski.

8. Knees rolled in, the rear ski is "slapped" into place and the skier is about to redistribute weight to the rear ski. Both skis are on edge here. To complete his run down the slope, the skier simply repeats the technique described in these photos.

9. Now let's look at the entire sequence from the rear, moving through it quickly so you get a feel for the pace. Do not worry too much about identifying each separate element of the turn, just focus on the rhythm and bear in mind that in its most essential form, linking turns means going from a weight commitment to full unweighting and back to a weight commitment again. In this photo, the skier plants his pole and unweights the uphill ski and begins to step forward with it.

10. *The turning ski has been placed forward, weight is transferred to it, and the rear (skier's right) ski is unweighted and shifting into place.*

11. *Now both skis are edged and weighted in the 70-30 forward-ski-to-rear-ski ratio. Knees and heels are rolled into the hill.*

12. *His first turn now completed, the skier plants his left pole to initiate a new turn.*

13. *The rear ski has been placed forward across the path of the left ski and weight has been transferred to it.*

14. *Now the left ski is brought in behind the turning ski and the skier begins again to redistribute weight.*

LESSON 7
SKIING THE STEEPS

Telemarking on steep slopes is an advanced technique that requires speed and hop-assisted unweighting. The ski-pole plant becomes a pivot for the skier, who also relies on heavy edge setting to negotiate the steep slope. In essence, this can be thought of as hopping from edge to edge. The turning radius is very narrow here. Skiing steeps in this fashion allows you to negotiate slopes that have been designed with mogul lines specifically challenging to alpine skiers.

The telemarker needs to rely on heavy angulation, radical unweighting, and a strong commitment during turn initiation on such terrain. Though all the basic telemarking techniques covered thus far are present in this radical telemarking, they are somewhat modified to create speed and power in the turns.

When skiing the steeps it is important to remember that the telemark turn emphasizes stability. Chances are that even skilled skiers will find themselves in situations where they are losing control. When this happens, you can regain control by riding out a turn or extending it by assuming the stable telemark position.

1. Begin a steep-slope turn by planting the pole and pushing away from it with the downhill ski. This can be thought of as "hop initiation."

2. Pivoting around the planted pole, the skier hops into a radical step initiation. This is the moment of unweighting that precedes a strong weight-and-edge commitment to the skier's right ski. The trailing ski is tucked up high by bending the knee, and the forward ski is moving forward to be placed across the slope.

3. *Here the skier has landed on the snow and is beginning to roll his knees into the slope. The edges are set very hard against the snow and weight is distributed immediately to both skis in the 70-30, front-rear ratio. The skier is already reaching for the next pole plant that will be the beginning of his next turn.*

4. The skier is airborne again, pivoting around his pole. The left ski is moving forward to take a heavy weight commitment and the right ski is tucking up.

5. The skier regains the snow, sets both skis on edge . . .

6. . . . and drops momentarily into the stable telemark position from which he will rise and push off into a new hop-initiated turn.

LESSON 8
TIPS ON MOGULS

How you handle a mogul field while skiing downhill is often the way in which you best define your style as a skier. The bumps and troughs are an open invitation to express yourself. The telemark turn typically is slower and requires a wider radius than a parallel or a stem-christy turn—but you can adjust your fundamental telemark technique to handle the narrow paths that moguls sometimes require.

Basically, you need to incorporate the hop-initiation of skiing steeps, discussed in the previous lesson, with the way in which you decide to address the terrain. In this lesson we will cover some basic mogul-skiing situations and offer some tips that will help you express yourself smoothly and stylishly on your telemark skis.

We will not go over each component of a turn in this lesson, for at this point you should have the developed necessary skills to recognize the dynamics of the telemark turn and know how to execute them. This lesson is for the advanced skier whose telemarking technique is well honed. We will confine comments to the most important aspects of what is happening in each photo.

Remember that you are likely at one time or another to lose balance and run into control problems with this fast skiing down a mogul field. If you need to bail out, you can simply extend a turn and ride it out to a stop in the stable telemark position or you can make a broad, sweeping traverse to slow up and regain control.

1. As in skiing steeps, hop turns are required when negotiating moguls; they help to get your long nordic skis around in time. Be sure to tuck the trailing ski high by bending the knee.

2. The skier has landed and dropped directly into a telemark stance, with both skis edged. The snow that is frequently scraped off mogul tops accumulates in "crud piles," which are excellent spots in which to land. They are shock absorbing and give good edge control.

3. Here the skier is planting his pole and hopping into a turn on the top downhill side of a bump . . .

4. . . . he is unweighted and tucking his rear ski up and the left ski is being brought forward . . .

5. . . . now the forward ski has been placed across the line of travel, rear ski is slapping into position, and the pole is being used as a pivot.

6. *Coming around the bump, the skier has both skies edged, and he carves into the trough in front of the bump.*

7. Now the skier is through the trough and planting his pole for negotiating the next mogul.

8. This photo of the skier a little farther down the hill on the same run illustrates how you can slide or side-slip on packed powder to gain a better angle for addressing an upcoming mogul.

9. Here the skier has finished a slight side-slip and is angulating and edging skis heavily to pull out of it and hop into a new turn off a bump.

CHAPTER 4

EQUIPMENT
MAINTENANCE

L ike all fine tools, your telemarking equipment requires a certain amount of care and upkeep. Proper maintenance of your equipment isn't hard, and it will add to your enjoyment and knowledge of the sport of telemark skiing. Tasks such as safety checks, boot care, ski-base treatments, and ski-edge tuning can all be performed before you go out, either at home or at a ski center's equipment shop. These operations require only a small amount of time and a few tools. In this chapter, we'll look at some guidelines for maintaining your telemark skis, boots, poles, and bindings. First, though, we stress this point: Check your gear every time you go out and tune it frequently. Take care of your equipment, and it'll take care of you.

SKI MAINTENANCE

Because your skis take the most punishment, they need the most care. What follows is a step-by-step, full treatment for your skis. This should be performed about once every month during the ski season or even more frequently if you ski more than twice a week. The treatment will greatly lengthen the life of your telemark skis, so it's worth the 40 minutes to one hour it takes to complete.

STEP 1: SETUP AND SCRAPING. Start by setting up one ski in a shop or home workbench vise, bottom up. Gather together the equipment you'll need: metal-tooth brush, metal file, metal scraper, edge tuner (a block of smooth stone), a true bar, plastic scraper, and glide wax. The glide wax can be either alpine or cross country glide wax; use one designated for the temperature range you expect to ski in—or you can use one of the new "universal" gliders.

Start by setting your metal scraper across your ski at a 90-degree angle from the metal edges. Look at how the scraper lines up across the width of the ski. If you notice that your ski is edge-high (that is, the

77

scraper rests on both metal edges with a concave space between the scraper and the plastic surface of the base), you won't need to scrape the base down. If, on the other hand, your scraper won't touch both edges at once, your ski is base-high (or convex), and it will need to be scraped down.

To scrape the base down, lay your scraper against the base, perpendicular to it, with your thumbs pressing against the center of the scraper. Working from tip to tail, scrape the base down. Hold the scraper at an angle and use only gentle pressure. Continue, removing base material from your scraper that accumulates after each pass, until the base is flush with the metal edges. Check this by holding the scraper perpendicular to the base and sighting down the base.

STEP 2: FILING EDGES. Once your base is flush with the metal edges, you may file the edges themselves. To do this, use a metal file. Note that when you use the file, you should work from tip to tail with the file set at an angle and the handle of the file oriented toward the tip of the ski (this is so the file's working surface is always pointed in the right direction). Keeping the file as flat on the ski as possible, stand toward the tail of the ski and draw the file back, down the ski. After every pass or two, use your wire brush to remove metal filings from the surface of the file. The number of strokes it takes to hone the edges depends upon how dull your edges are. Judge by feel; a well-honed edge shouldn't cut your finger but it should be fairly sharp.

Once the bottoms of your metal edges are honed, proceed to the sides of the edges. Set your ski sideways in the vise and secure it. Then, keeping the file handle pointed toward the tip of the ski, draw the file down the ski, moving from tip to tail. This should give your edge a fairly sharp feel and bright, shiny appearance after a few strokes.

It isn't necessary to produce a razor edge all the way down the ski. The most important section for your on-snow turning ability is directly underfoot, a few inches in front of your binding and behind the heelplate. However, you should file all the way down the length of the metal edges to remove any irregularities. Again, check your work after every two passes or so; look for a brighter shine on the edge of the newly filed area. There are two important exceptions to this: Once the edges are sharp, you will need to dull the fronts and backs of the edges slightly. Dulling the fronts and backs adds stability to your skis; if these areas are too sharp, your skis will tend to bite prematurely, making initiation of the telemark turn more difficult. To dull the edges, run your file over them a few times at a 45-degree angle to the base. Dull about three to four inches (about a hand's width) from the shovel of the ski down and from three to four inches from the end of the tail—again, working with tip-to-tail strokes.

Occasionally an edge may be damaged by a rock or a sharp blow,

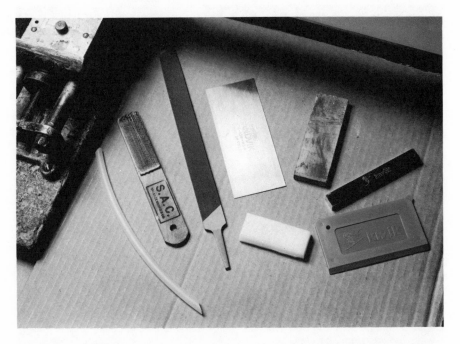

Only a few tools are needed for basic ski care. From left to right are a stick of of P-tex, wire brush, flat file, metal scraper, edge-tuning stone, true bar, and plastic scraper. Center: a cake of glide wax.

producing a burr. Remove burrs with an edge stone. Holding the damaged ski upright, set the stone flat against the edge and rub vigorously along the edge bottom. Turn the ski to the side and repeat the procedure until the burr is removed.

STEP 3: GLIDE WAXING. For maximum performance on the slopes, you should glide wax your skis regularly. Unless you're skiing on abrasive snow or you ski particularly hard, you probably won't need to glide wax every time you go out.

You should, however, check your bases every time you get set to ski. If it's been a while since you waxed, you will notice that the base has a slightly whitish aspect to it. This means that your old wax has worn off and it's time to rewax.

To glide wax your skis, you'll need an extra piece of equipment: a waxing iron. Ideally, you should use a special iron designed for ski waxing, because (in the plug-in variety) it heats to the right temperature and has an appropriate shape for the job. If you don't have a plug-in waxing iron, you can heat your iron with a propane torch. Many people, though, simply swipe an old clothes iron from the laundry room at home and use this. An old iron is fine, too; if you have a choice, use the

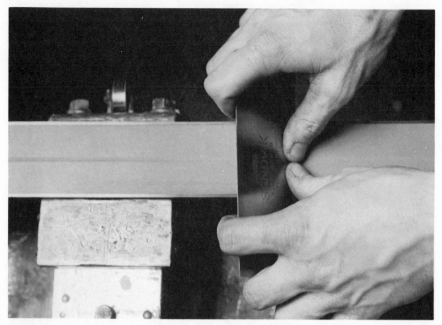

Begin to tune by scraping down excess material on the plastic base. Scrape gently, always moving from tip to tail.

Sight down the base of the ski after every few strokes. Look for an even line across the edge of the scraper. The base is ready when flush with the metal edges.

To file metal edge bottoms, hold your file with the handle oriented toward the ski's tip. Draw the file down the ski, working always from tip to tail.

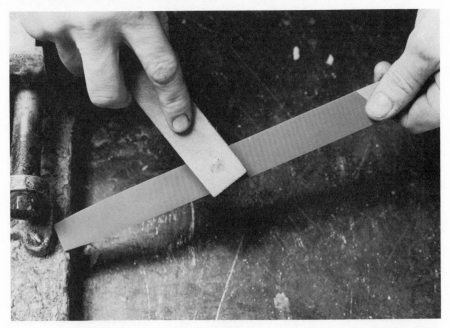

After every few strokes, clean metal shavings from the file with a stiff wire brush.

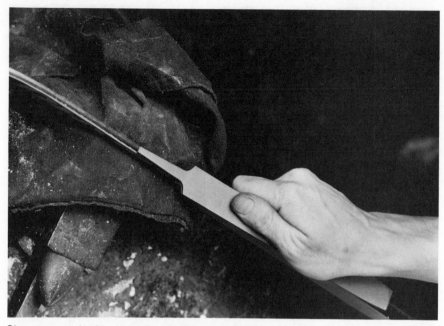

Sharpen metal edge sides by setting your ski sideways in the vise (protect the ski with a cloth, as shown). Draw the file down the edge, handle pointed toward the tip.

Once the edges are sharp, dull the shovel and tip areas slightly. File each edge gently at a 45-degree angle.

To repair metal burrs on the edges, hold the ski upright. Set an edge-tuning stone against the underside of the metal edge and rub vigorously.

Repeat the process on the outside of the metal edge until the burr is removed.

old nonsteam types (the holes on the bottom surface of steam irons tend to collect wax).

Let's assume for the moment that you're using an old clothes iron. First, check to see that your ski base is clean and dry and doesn't have any old wax sticking to it. In the meantime, heat your iron to a medium setting. Once it's up to temperature, hold it upside down (front tip pointing downward) above the ski base and to one side or the other of the central groove. Place your cake of wax against the iron.

The wax will rapidly melt and drip onto the base. As it's melting, move the iron and wax down the length of the ski, dripping all the way. Then repeat the process on the other side of the ski's central groove. You don't need to cover the entire base with drips; a thin line of drips on either side of the groove will suffice.

When you have finished the dripping, put your cake of wax aside and rub the still-hot iron over the base until the hot wax has spread over the width of the base. Ironing in wax like this achieves two things. First, it assures a smooth, even coat of wax over the whole base. Second, it causes pores in the base material to expand slightly, letting them absorb the wax and, thus, retain the glide wax longer. Once you have a smooth coat of wax over the entire running surface of the ski, set that ski aside and let the wax cool—about 25 minutes (you can wax the other ski while this one cools).

Once your glide wax is cool, you may scrape it down to a thin layer. Use your plastic scraper for this job, because your metal one may dig into the base—something you want to avoid at this juncture. Set it against the ski base, perpendicular to the metal edges (as you did when you scraped the base down), with your thumbs set against the center of the scraper. Again, working from tip to tail, scrape down the excess wax. Remove all excess wax from the scraper and the sides of your ski after each stroke. When you have a thin layer of glide wax remaining, use the rounded edge of your scraper to remove wax from the central groove of the base. This is particularly important; if excess wax remains in the central groove, your skis will not track properly on the slopes. When finished scraping, buff your wax job with a waxing cork or soft rag, always stroking from tip to tail as you work.

Sometimes when skiing, you may hit a rock or other obstruction just underneath the snow. This can produce a sizable gouge in the plastic ski base. Fortunately, most such gouges are easily repaired by using essentially the same techniques you employ when you scrape and wax your skis.

To fix a gouge, you first need a stick of P-tex. This is the plastic used in most ski bases, and it's readily available in repair-kit-size sticks. You can even find P-tex in the color of your base material.

Start by securing the damaged ski in a vise, bottom side up. Carefully

To glide wax your skis, place a ski upside down in the vise. When the waxing iron is hot, hold it over the ski and place a cake of glide wax against it. Move down base .

Iron the wax into the base by stroking the iron along the length of the base. Then set the base aside to cool for half an hour.

When wax is cool, scrape it down with a plastic scraper. Hold the scraper at an angle and clean it after each stroke.

Clear the central groove of wax with the rounded corner of the scraper. Be careful not to scrape base material.

Buff your wax job after scraping with a cork or soft rag.

Use a stick of P-tex to repair gouges in a plastic base. Start by lighting one end of the stick to liquefy the plastic filler.

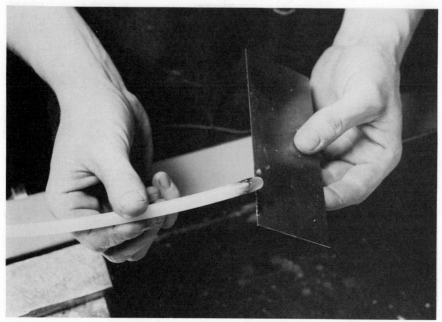

If carbon deposits appear on the P-tex, scrape them off with the edge of a metal scraper.

Draw the tip of the softened repair stick backward along the gouge. If the stick cools, relight, clean, and draw it down the base again until finished.

When the filler material has cooled, scrape it down with a metal scraper. Then scrape down the repair job until the true bar indicates it is flush with the base.

cut away or sand down any ridges of plastic in the gouge, then clean the surface of the ski. Next, light one end of the stick of P-tex by holding a match to it until a small blue flame appears (keep the stick pointed flame side down, away from the ski base). If carbon begins to build up on the P-tex stick, scrape it against the edge of your metal scraper.

Now you're ready to fill the gouge with melting plastic. Start your work at the far end of the gouge, keeping the small blue flame at the end of the P-tex stick close to the base (the closer the flame stays to the base, the easier it is to keep the plastic filler pure and carbon-free). As you let hot plastic drip into the gouge, draw your P-tex stick back slowly over the base, until the entire gouge has been filled.

Let the P-tex set. When it is cool to the touch, scrape it down with your metal scraper, just as you would ordinary base material, until your repair job is as smooth as the rest of the base.

STEP 4: CLEANING THE BASE. Once you've finished your base repair or before you wax your skis, you must remove any dirt or old wax that remains on the ski bases. Some people like to use heat for this procedure, warming up the wax with a waxing iron, then quickly rubbing it off with a cloth towel. For better results, though, it's often faster and easier to use chemical solvents. Commercial wax remover is excellent for this purpose. Soak a cloth towel in the wax remover, then rub the towel against the base until all old wax is removed. Then rewax your skis, as described above.

BOOT MAINTENANCE

Well-maintained telemark boots are crucial to your comfort and safety on the slopes. Unlike telemark skis, though, they require little in the way of special tools and materials. A few safety checks before you go skiing, plus occasional treatments, should be sufficient for boot care throughout the winter months.

Most telemark boots are made of leather, and so must be water-proofed from time to time. One solution is a good silicone-based water-proofing agent applied to your boots the night before you plan to ski. Boot oils and leather conditioners are also recommended. When you waterproof your boots, make sure that they are completely dry and clean (use a small brush or bootblack's brush to remove mud or grit on the surface of the leather before you apply waterproofer). And choose one type of waterproofer—silicone or oil—for your boots and stick with it through further applications.

Here's one rule of boot care that is easy to break but is one of the most important rules: Don't dry your boots on a radiator or other heat source. This can make the leather tough or brittle, resulting in less comfort and shorter boot life. In addition, boots placed on a radiator can be a fire hazard. If placed in an area with good air circulation, at room temperature, most boots will dry sufficiently overnight for you to ski comfortably in them the next day. And remember to loosen laces and open boots up as wide as possible after a hard day's skiing to dry the inside layers as well.

The rest of boot care consists of prevention and regular inspection. If your boots have laces, check these before you go out (and remember to waterproof them along with the boots themselves). Also, check the eyelets of the boots for signs of stress or detachment and repair them at the first sign of damage. If your boots have Velcro fasteners, keep them free of snow and dirt and brush them clean every now and then.

The soles of your boots merit special consideration. It's here that most boots first show wear, especially near the toe box and along the ball of your foot. You may begin to notice, for example, a little lateral sloppiness on high-stress turns or accumulations of snow or ice between soles and the sidewalls of your bindings. Lateral sloppiness indicates that the pin holes of your boots may be wearing out: These should be fitted with metal inserts, or reinforced by a metal plate bolted to the bottom of the sole. Kits for this purpose are available at many ski shops. Space between soles and bindings means that the soles have worn down from repeated up-and-down friction against the bindings. If the wear is extensive, replacement of the soles is the best course (some nylon-coated bindings minimize wear against soles, and, thus, prevent or delay costly repairs).

POLES AND BINDINGS

Because both poles and bindings are structurally simple, maintenance and repair of these items is easy. To check your telemark poles, think first of the maximum pressure points on them: the straps, baskets, and tips. Straps take the heaviest beating, especially if they are made of leather. Look for signs of stretching and frayed edges where the straps meet the grips. If signs of strain are evident, replace the straps immediately; it's possible, of course, to knot the ends of a damaged strap together, but this is only good as an emergency measure and can be pretty frustrating on the slopes. Other repair methods, such as stitching together a damaged strap, only postpone the inevitable. If you're the type who wears a strap down quickly, consider using nylon models. They may be a bit less comfortable than leather but will last longer.

Pole baskets that are worn out can be easily replaced on most models. As with straps, nylon or plastic models will last longer than metal baskets with leather webbing. And pole tips, although quite strong, have been known to snap off with a single unfortunate pole plant. Replacement tips are available, but many poles simply won't take them. In this case, it's a good idea to prevent trouble from the start: When you purchase a pair of poles be sure that they will accept new tips and that your dealer carries these items.

Although telemark pole shafts are sturdy (especially the aluminum-alloy models), they can bend or break in a fall. Some skiers are able to find a metal worker who can weld the shaft together at the break, although its future sturdiness may be a question mark. Fiberglass poles are brittle, and a break generally means a total loss. In this case, do what they do in Vermont: Buy a new pair of poles and give the unshattered pole from your first pair to an older person for use as a walking-stick during the icy winter months.

Bindings are even tougher than poles and need little care beyond routine cleaning. There's one important exception: the bail of the binding. Under the heavy turning stress of telemark skiing, bails can pop out, bend, or even break. Borrow a leaf from the book of backcountry skiers to insure against bail trouble and carry an extra bail along with you to the slopes. Most models of telemark bindings have bails that can be quickly replaced. This is another example of an ounce of prevention: Check with your dealer when you purchase your bindings and buy an extra set of bails to stow away in your fanny pack for fast repair on the slopes.

AFTERWORD

Now that you've had the opportunity to read this book, and to practice some of the techniques of telemark skiing outlined in the lessons, we feel it is appropriate to stress certain important points—tips that will keep your learning curve headed upward. Even if you haven't yet tried some of the on-snow techniques, pausing here for a moment should be helpful. We'd like to cover a couple of things that you can take with you beyond the specifics of the lessons in this book—material that forms the basis of a sort of continuing education. These are reflections on telemark skiing, it's true. But they also form an approach to the learning process itself.

The first point is something you can keep in mind whenever you're at a ski slope: Watching accomplished telemarkers is a lesson in itself. In his first book about learning a sport, *Inner Tennis*, Tim Galway relates this point to a central fact: The human mind and body are incredibly versatile, and learn to relate familiar practices to new techniques as you try a new sport. After all, your mind sends, cancels, and modifies innumerable messages to muscles everyday, all day long, even when you do simple things (such as turning the pages of this book). Your brain issues a command, then a new one, and the muscles respond with astonishing accuracy. Learning the telemark turn, then, is really nothing more than adapting old knowledge to a new situation. The point of this brief digression into human physiology is this: Think about the telemark turn ... your mind already knows how to tell your muscles to bend the knees, roll them in, and so on—these are all simple tasks, well known to your mind and muscles; you already knew how to do these things before you first tried telemarking.

So why does learning something new, such as telemarking, always seem somewhat difficult? Well, Galway suggests (and we agree), that you get uptight because you start cluttering the even flow of messages to your muscles with a bunch of new messages—messages like: "Hope I don't fall," "Hope I'm doing this right," "Hope no one's watching,"

"Hope I'm learning as fast as Bob is."

In *Inner Tennis*, Galway, a tennis pro, describes experimenting with students who had never played tennis before. Without a word of instruction, he hit a number of forehand shots and asked the students to watch carefully as he did so. After his demonstration, he asked the students to do what he had just done. He had an unusually high rate of success in teaching that stroke to the group of newcomers to the sport. What was different about this, when compared to conventional teaching methods? An absence of verbal instruction. The "message load" the students were asked to carry was comparatively uncluttered. But what they did have in large measure was a clear mental imprint of the right way to hit a forehand stroke. By simply watching, then letting the body use familiar physical actions in a new way, the student builds upon the mind's ability to imitate, and the body's ability to adapt to change.

In telemarking, as in tennis or other active sports, it is possible to learn a great deal just by observing an accomplished athlete. You're making an imprint—your mind is absorbing an image—that has value in itself, without being accompanied by conscious intellectual interpretation. Naturally, you'll sometimes find yourself focusing narrowly on how, for example, a fine skier initiates his turn. That's fine—a natural curiosity. But in a basic and pleasing way, you can learn every time you simply watch a good skier execute his turns.

Many ski instructors dealt with just this issue of "cluttering" mental messages before Galway expressly interpreted it in a teaching context. These instructors saw that there was one overwhelmingly obstructive mental message that kept many skiers from learning both downhill and cross country techniques—that feeling of "Yipes! I hope I don't fall!" They dealt with it very simply—by teaching their students how to fall. Once a student learned that he could fall and not get hurt, the fear was substantially lessened, and the mental message was no longer an obstacle to learning ski technique. So, if a fear of falling starts to interfere with your telemarking learning process, take a break and fall down a few times. With a little practice you'll become quite good at it! Use common sense and you'll see how easy it is to go from upright to sitting on the snow without incurring an injury.

The "imprint" approach to learning is one of the reasons we chose to use as few words and as many photos as possible in this book. Though we have imparted verbally the specifics of each lesson in the technique section, it can sometimes be helpful simply to page through the photographs of a specific lesson you may be having trouble with. Just for a while, ignore the captions; try to imagine the sequence photos as a moving picture, and think about what it feels like to be doing what the skier in the photo is doing.

This brings us back to the first point—that you should observe good telemarkers on the slopes. Beyond using the photos in this book, take advantage of watching accomplished telemark skiers when you're on the slopes. Then it will be much easier to appreciate and make use of the captions we've provided when you return to them at a later date.

A second important point about learning to telemark with the greatest efficiency is: Don't to be too hard on yourself. It's not an easy sport to learn—which is probably why it has interested so many of us to begin with. Patience pays off. Perhaps you will want to use this book to set up a program for yourself that recognizes realistic expectations. Then, if you find yourself becoming discouraged, refer to your program and see if you're not asking too much of yourself too soon. (Incidentally, we are the first to point that there is no replacement for lessons from professionals. This book is an excellent adjunct to personal lessons, if they are available in your area.)

Thirdly, although ski magazines so often run dramatic photos of people telemarking waist-deep powder in exotic ski destinations or jumping huge cornices, we see no reason why telemarking shouldn't be considered a sport available to all skiers, since it doesn't have to be an "extreme skiing" experience. In fact, it is a fine family sport. If you ski with your family, you can all have fun telemarking or learning to telemark. With children, for instance, the lessons in this book provide ample opportunity to create fun games to enhance the learning process. Telemark traverses (to take but one example) can be turned into a relay, where one child traverses to a bandanna hung on a ski pole or another pre-placed "flag" on your slope, picks it up, and relays it to his brother or sister who waits at the end of the next traverse. When teaching children to ski, some noteworthy instructors believe that a skill foundation should first be laid in cross country—diagonal striding, and so on—before moving on to learning alpine skiing. If a child became skilled in cross country skiing, then learned telemarking when ready, and then moved on to acquire alpine downhill skills—now *there* would be a complete skier!

One last point: Putting "challenge" and "tradition" and similar high-minded thoughts aside for the moment, we think telemarking is just plain fun. It can be just as much fun while learning as it can be after you're an accomplished telemarker. In fact, enjoying the learning process is fundamental to progress in learning. Perhaps we like the sport so much because the fun seems so ubiquitous among its practictioners, too. We'll close here as Dick Hall, founder and director of NATO (North American Telemark Organization), closes a recent press release to us: "Ski hard, play fair, have fun."

INDEX